BONDED *Love*

How God's Love Shines Through Imperfect Relationships

STUDY GUIDE

Damone Paul Johnson

Copyright ©2023 by Damone Paul Johnson, Albany, New York
www.damonepauljohnson.com

All rights reserved. Except as permitted under the U.S. Copyright Act of 1976, no part of this publication may be reproduced, distributed or transmitted in any form or by any means, or stored in a database or retrieval system, without the prior written permission of the author or publisher. Published by King Jesus Press LLC. www.kingjesuspress.com

ISBN: 978-1-7368046-3-6

Library of Congress Control Number: 2023906573

Unless otherwise indicated, Scripture verses quoted are from the King James Version of the Bible, public domain.

Scripture quotations taken from the New King James Version®. Copyright ©1982 by Thomas Nelson. Used by permission. All rights reserved.

THE HOLY BIBLE, NEW INTERNATIONAL VERSION®, NIV® Copyright ©1973, 1978, 1984, 2011 by Biblica, Inc.® Used by permission. All rights reserved worldwide.

Scripture quotations marked (NLT) are taken from the Holy Bible, New Living Translation, copyright ©1996, 2004, 2007, 2013, 2015 by Tyndale House Foundation. Used by permission of Tyndale House Publishers, Inc., Carol Stream, Illinois 60188. All rights reserved.

CONTENTS

Introduction .... I.

Week 1 1
Almost Doesn't Count

Week 2 9
It's a Thin Line Between Love and Hate

Week 3 19
Let Me Tell You How This Mama Made It

Week 4 27
The Blessed Man

Week 5 35
Before We Separate, Let's Communicate

Week 6 45
I'm in the Family Too

Week 7 53
Lessons from Young Lovers

Week 8 61
That Kind of Love

Week 9 69
Endless Love

Week 10 77
Love's Power Over All Things

Week 11 85
Love's Power Over Time

Week 12 95
The Thrill is Gone

About the Author 105

Other Books 106

INTRODUCTION

Bonding is another word for joining something to hold it together, strengthen it, or repair it. When we look at romantic and other love relationships, we know there are often cracks in need of repair. Through the book, "Bonded Love: How God's Love Shines Through Imperfect Relationships," you learn just how repair is possible. You also learn how God's love remains with you throughout all of life's trials and tribulations.

The "Bonded Love Study Guide" is a complement to that book and allows readers to go deeper into the lessons designed to walk you through broken relationships and situations to reveal just how God's love shines through. It is designed for group study - church Bible study, marriage ministries, book clubs, small cell groups in the home, virtual study with friends or family, etc. - or individual study for those looking for intimate, alone time with God.

Getting the Most Out of This Study Guide

Each lesson in this 12-week study guide correlates with the chapters from the book. All information is based off a series of sermons I preached at Metropolitan NTM Baptist Church where I serve as senior pastor. To get the most out of this study, I recommend you read the book first.

For Group Study: Each week has a key Scripture, focal verse, overview, lesson, questions for discussion, closing prayer, and homework. Open each session with prayer. Different volunteers should read each section aloud. When you get to the questions for discussion section, the facilitator should allow ample time for participants to think about and jot down their answers.

Then, open the conversation to discuss responses. Each week ends with a closing prayer. Although it is a group study, the prayers are written in the first person because it should be personal for each

of you to help strengthen your bond with God. Take time throughout the week to complete the homework. It will not be checked in class as it is personal, but the facilitator should use the start of the class time to encourage homework completion. You should also answer any questions for homework if time did not allow you to complete them in class.

For Individual Study: Each week has a key Scripture, focal verse, overview, lesson, questions for discussion, closing prayer, and homework. Open each lesson with prayer and ask God to reveal himself to you and increase your understanding of the lesson. You do not have time constraints as you would in a group session, so pace yourself according to your own abilities and schedule. If you are studying with a spouse at home – which I recommend if you are married – take turns reading each section. When you get to the questions, answer as honestly and thoroughly as you can. Each lesson ends with a closing prayer. If you want, you can add to it based on what you have gleaned from the lesson. Take time throughout the week to complete the homework. If you have more time in the week, you could do two lessons instead of one, making this a six-week study for you instead of 12.

We are blessed to be a blessing to someone else. Be sure to share with others how this lesson has impacted you when you are done and encourage them to read these materials as well. I pray this study greatly enriches the relationships in your life and draws you closer to God's bonded love.

Week 1

ALMOST DOESN'T COUNT

Key Scripture: Genesis 21:14-17

Focal Verse: "And God heard the voice of the lad; and the angel of God called to Hagar out of heaven, and said unto her, What aileth thee, Hagar? fear not; for God hath heard the voice of the lad where he is." – *vs. 17*

Overview:

In this study, we will:

- Examine what happens when we step outside of God's will for our lives
- Recognize how an "almost" situation is not your finale
- Understand how God still keeps us even when we go through hard times

Lesson:

God's promises often sound so far-fetched to our carnal selves, they are hardly believable. Sometimes, they are even laughable. This is the scene we find in the book of Genesis where we have 90-year-old Abraham - whom God promised would have a son by his wife and be a father of many nations – and his 80-year-old wife, Sarah, who is barren. Since Sarah was beyond child-bearing age, she decided to help God out by implementing her own plan and procedure to manifest God's promise. She gave her husband permission to sleep with her Egyptian servant,

Hagar, so that Sarah could have children through her since she did not have any of her own. Abraham agreed, and Hagar had a son named Ishmael. Ten years after God promised Abraham a son through his wife, Sarah miraculously became pregnant and gave birth to a son named Isaac. As you can imagine, this is where the family dynamics got a little messy. Sarah – now with her promised child – no longer wanted Hagar and Ishmael around. Sarah did not want Ishmael to be an heir with Isaac. And besides, she caught Ishmael mocking Isaac, which angered her. Abraham sent Hagar and their son Ishmael away, just as Sarah wanted.

Read Genesis 21:14-17

Questions for Discussion:

1. How can you recognize God's voice when He is speaking?

   _____
   _____
   _____
   _____
   _____

2. Do you find it difficult to wait on God's promises to come to pass, just as Sarah did?

   _____
   _____
   _____
   _____
   _____

3. Sarah laughed in disbelief when she heard that she was going to have a son. Then, when Isaac was born, she laughed again, this time in amazement. Does this ever happen to you?

_____
_____
_____
_____
_____

4. Often, we may feel inadequate because of a lack, whether it is a lack of education, money, good health, or – in Abraham and Sarah's case - the ability to birth a child. How can you invite God in to help you deal with your feelings of inadequacy?

_____
_____
_____
_____
_____

5. God was very clear in Genesis 17:16 when he told Abraham that He would give him a son through his wife, Sarah. Why do you think he went along with Sarah's plan instead of waiting on God's plan?

_____
_____
_____
_____
_____

6. Have you ever gotten ahead of God to create your own plan and procedures in your life? If so, what were the results? What lessons have you learned from it?

_____
_____
_____
_____
_____

7. There is a lesson in the story of Abraham, Sarah and Hagar on blended families, which is prevalent in society today. What advice would you give to Abraham on dealing with a blended family? Advice to Hagar? Advice to Sarah?

_____
_____
_____
_____
_____

8. Hagar found herself wandering in the wilderness aimlessly without direction, and her provisions had run out. Her whole existence was tied to a man who kicked her and their son out of his life. Can you relate to Hagar's struggle in the wilderness? If so, explain.

_____
_____
_____
_____
_____

9. In this lesson, we also see a son, Ishmael, who was separated from his father, Abraham. Too often, we see fatherless households today. What effect does this have on single mothers? The children left behind? The communities?

_____
_____
_____
_____
_____

10. While in the wilderness, Hagar and Ishmael almost died. We too, encounter so many situations in our lives where we almost died, almost lost our house, almost lost our minds, almost got fired, almost got a divorce, etc., but God heard our voice. What are some examples where God preserved you even through hard times?

_____
_____
_____
_____
_____

Closing Prayer:

Father God, I worship you for being El-Shaddai, God Almighty. Thank you for your word you have left on record to guide me. This study has been a blessing, and I pray I continue to dwell on all the lessons I've learned. Forgive me, Father, for the times I have sidestepped your will and did my own thing. Help me to serve you faithfully and live a blameless life, as you have instructed Abraham to do.

Please help me to stay steadfast in waiting on your promises. Help me to know your voice. Help me to distinguish your will from mine. I pray, LORD, that you keep me on the narrow way. But if I should stray and become separated from you, I pray you protect me along my journey. Please show up in the places where I ought not be and set me back on the right path. Father God, in those "almost" times, I pray I never give up. I know those "almost" times don't count because you give me just what I need to survive and thrive. Continue to keep me bonded to you through your love and grace. In Jesus' name, I pray. Hallelujah and amen.

Homework:

Use the following blank pages to journal your thoughts on this lesson throughout the week. Below are some tools to use as writing prompts to help you get started.

Answer this question - How can I apply this lesson to my everyday life?

Make a list of promises God has made to you. Cross out the ones that have already come to pass. Pray for direction over the remaining promises.

LET'S JOURNAL!

Week 2

IT'S A THIN LINE BETWEEN LOVE AND HATE

Key Scripture: 2 Samuel 13

Focal Verses: "And it came to pass after this, that Absalom the son of David had a fair sister, whose name was Tamar; and Amnon the son of David loved her. Then Amnon hated her exceedingly; so that the hatred wherewith he hated her was greater than the love wherewith he had loved her." - *vs. 1 and 15*

Overview:

In this lesson, we will:

- Get a clear understanding of what love is and what it is not
- Learn to consider our position in the kingdom of God before committing actions that are displeasing to God
- Understand self-love as a first step in loving others

Lesson:

Producer Dick Wolf created a television show called Law & Order: SVU. The SVU stands for Special Victims Unit because the detectives in this police drama investigate sexually oriented crimes including rape. Although a fictional television show, the storylines are very much real for a lot of women who have endured the painful experience of being raped and sexually abused. This type of behavior did not begin with the Law & Order franchise, though.

In the Book of 2 Samuel, 13th chapter, we see this scene play out thousands of years earlier. King David's son, Amnon, was so obsessed and in love with his half-sister, Tamar, and it made him feel sick. The term lovesickness is appropriate in this story; referring to an affliction that can produce negative feelings when deeply in love, during the absence of a loved one, or when love is not reciprocated. Tamar, also a child of King David's, was a beautiful princess with her innocence intact. She was a virgin. Amnon's friend and cousin, Jonadab, helped him devise a scheme to get Tamar into his bedroom. Listening to this foolish advice, Amnon pretended to be sick and asked King David if Tamar could fix his favorite meal in front of him and feed it to him by his bedside. The king agreed, and Tamar did as she was instructed to do by her father. However, when she got close enough to feed him, Amnon grabbed her forcefully and raped her, despite her rejections. After Amnon brought shame unto Tamar, his love quickly turned to hate, and he threw her out.

Read 2 Samuel 13.

Questions For Discussion:

1. What is your definition of love?

_____

_____

_____

_____

_____

2. Based on these definitions of love below, describe Amnon's behavior.

Love is not 50-50. Love is giving 100 percent to someone.

Amnon's behavior: _____

_____

_____

_____

_____

Love is wanting the best for another person.

Amnon's behavior: _____

_____

_____

_____

_____

Love is an act of your will; consciously deciding to love someone positively and unconditionally and not from a place of temporary emotions and feelings.

Amnon's behavior: _____

_____

_____

_____

_____

Love is assessing the needs of others and meeting those needs.

Amnon's behavior: _____

_____

_____

_____

_____

Love is about commitment.

Amnon's behavior: _____

_____

_____

_____

_____

3. How does one go from love to hate?

_____
_____
_____
_____
_____

4. When you are dealing with love in relationships (regardless of the type of relationship: partners, parents, children, friends), where do you go to seek advice on love?

_____
_____
_____
_____
_____

5. How can you tell whether you are getting sound advice or foolish advice on love?

_____
_____
_____

_____

_____

6. Tamar, Amnon and Absalom were a part of a royal family. With that came great responsibilities including proper conduct. As Christians, we too, are a part of a royal family – the body of Christ. What happens when others witness our actions that do not align with God?

_____

_____

_____

_____

_____

7. When you know who you are (not the fake version of yourself you show people on social media, in church, or other areas), it should affect what you do and allow others to do to you. What role should our Christian walk play in our actions toward others, especially those we say we love?

_____

_____

_____

_____

_____

8. What impact does low self-esteem have on how we treat others? On how we treat ourselves?

_____

_____

_____

_____

_____

9. What are some ways we can incorporate self-love in our lives?

_____

_____

_____

_____

_____

Closing Prayer:

Father God, I worship you for being omniscient. Because you are an all-knowing God, you know when I have not always been loving toward the people whom I say I love. I pray for your forgiveness, in the name of Jesus. I thank you for your grace that keeps me, even when I don't deserve to be kept. Thank you for showing me the greatest example of love by giving us your Son, Jesus. LORD, please help me to be patient, kind, humble and hopeful always. Please remove any fake or phoniness within me so I may be my authentic, loving self. In Jesus' name, I pray. Hallelujah and amen.

Homework:

Use the following blank pages to journal your thoughts on this lesson throughout the week. Below are some tools to use as writing prompts to help you get started.

Answer this question - How can I apply this lesson to my everyday life?

Write a letter to Absalom's sister, Tamar, to encourage her after her traumatic experience. Assure her that the assault was not her fault and give her hope for a brighter future. For some, this lesson is personal. Eighty-one percent of women and 43 percent of men in the U.S. reported experiencing some form of sexual harassment and/or assault in their lifetime, according to the National Sexual Violence Resource Center. If this is your story, write a letter to yourself about your traumatic experience, speaking life into yourself where you may feel pain.

LET'S JOURNAL!

Week 3

LET ME TELL YOU HOW THIS MAMA MADE IT

Key Scripture: I Kings 17:1-16

Focal Verse: "For thus saith the LORD God of Israel, The barrel of meal shall not waste, neither shall the cruse of oil fail, until the day that the LORD sendeth rain upon the earth." – *vs. 14*

Overview:

In this lesson, you will:

- Understand the importance of listening to the word of the LORD
- How change is sometimes necessary to get us to the next level in life
- How God can provide even in difficult times
- The benefit of putting God first

Lesson:

When the COVID-19 crisis struck in 2020, it had a ripple effect throughout our nation. The supply chain was broken, affecting everything from auto parts to food. People lost jobs, and some businesses even had to close permanently. To help struggling families get the food they desperately needed, the government increased SNAP (Supplemental Nutrition Assistance Program) benefits for eligible individuals and households. This was a great relief for those who had food insecurities.

But, the widow in the village of Zarephath, found in I Kings 17, did not have a government program to rely on during her nation's crisis; famine caused by a drought. All she had in her house was a handful of flour left in a jar and a little cooking oil in the bottom of a jug. Feeling defeated and hopeless, this widow was gathering sticks for a fire to make her last meal for her son and herself. She knew that without food, they were surely going to die. But, help was on the way. God instructed the prophet Elijah to go to Zarephath where a widow woman was going to feed him. She took the scraps she had and made food, but fed God's prophet first, as he instructed her to do. Because of her obedience, God made sure there was always enough flour and oil left in the containers. He made her *last,* last.

Read I Kings 17:1-16

Questions for Discussion:

1. Elijah had provisions, even in a drought, because God sustained him (vs. 6). But, his location was not his final destination, even though he was comfortable there. God told him to go to Zarephath. Think of a time when God told you to shift to something new. Did you obey? If so, was it easy for you or difficult to change course? Explain.

_____

_____

_____

_____

2. If you could write an alternate version of this story, what would have happened if Elijah did *not* listen to God but stayed where he was by the brook Cherith?

_____
_____
_____
_____
_____

3. Give an example in biblical history where someone disobeyed God's word. What was the result?

_____
_____
_____
_____
_____

4. The widow was experiencing dire circumstances in her life. She had given up because she saw no way out. We too, go through periods of drought in our lives: financial droughts, relationship droughts, career droughts, etc.

What are some of the positive ways you cope when you experience situations with no signs of relief in sight?

_____
_____
_____
_____
_____

5. With barely enough ingredients to make a meal for her son and herself, the widow agreed to feed Elijah first. Do you find it difficult to give in this generous way, especially to strangers? Explain.

_____
_____
_____
_____
_____

6. Elijah told the widow to *fear not* because she was concerned about her lack of resources. He assured this mama that she would not run out of food because the LORD God of Israel said so. What, if anything, keeps you from trusting God's word?

_____

_____

_____

_____

_____

7. As a struggling parent, how did the widow benefit from following the instructions God gave her through Elijah?

_____

_____

_____

_____

_____

Closing Prayer:

Father God, I worship you today for being Jehovah-Jireh. You are my provider. I recognize that all things come from you. Even when I act as a disobedient child, you still give me what I need. Please forgive me, LORD, for my shortcomings, my trust issues, and my bad memory when it comes to your promises. Let me not forget all the ways you have provided for me in the past. Thank you, Father God, for constantly stretching my resources, even when I don't see a path forward. Just like you did for the widow woman, I pray for your continued provisions so they may not run out. Help me to put you first always. In Jesus' name, I pray. Hallelujah and amen.

Homework:

Use the following blank pages to journal your thoughts on this lesson throughout the week. Below are some tools to use as writing prompts to help you get started.

Answer this question - How can I apply this lesson to my everyday life?

What can you do to contribute to the work of God?

LET'S JOURNAL!

Week 4

THE BLESSED MAN

Key Scripture: Psalm 128

Focal Verse: "Behold, that thus shall the man be blessed that feareth the LORD." – *vs. 4*

Overview:

In this lesson, you will:

- Understand what it truly means to be blessed, defying the world's definition of blessed
- Identify areas in your life where you are blessed
- Understand the importance of being productive and gain knowledge in how to do so

Lesson:

Fred Hammond, a popular gospel artist, had a hit song in 1995 titled, "We're Blessed." The first verse says:

Since thou hast walked uprightly, as a light in a dark land
Since thou hast placed in thine heart, all the LORD'S commands
He's set thee above nations, He's cast thine enemies away
He's standing up within thee, so let me hear you say

Fred set the stage for his audience to understand the reason behind the blessing - *because thou hast walked uprightly.* Then, in the chorus, he described all the ways we are blessed:

We're blessed in the city
We're blessed in the field
We're blessed when we come and when we go
We cast down every stronghold
Sickness and poverty must cease
For the devil is defeated
We are blessed

This song, inspired by Scripture in Deuteronomy 28, echoes the description in Psalm 128 of how to be blessed. The first verse in Psalm 128 says everyone must fear the LORD and walk in His ways. If you look at it closely, there are two different ingredients in that verse: 1. Fear the LORD and 2. Walk in His ways. You would not bake a cake with sugar *or* flour. No, you must use sugar *and* flour if you want it to come out right. As such, you cannot be blessed by doing one or the other. Fearing the LORD does you no good if you choose not to walk in His ways. But, when you do, you will reap great benefits: you will produce and enjoy the fruits of your labor, your home will flourish, and your future will be prosperous as well.

Read Psalm 128

Questions for Discussion:

1. Christians often greet one another with a declaration of being blessed. "How are you?" "I'm blessed and highly favored!" What does being blessed mean to you?

_____

_____

_____

2. What do you think being blessed means to non-Christians?

___

___

___

___

___

3. Blessings can be described in two ways. One of them is *barack* – meaning God showers blessings on you because you have a connection with Him. You depend on Him only and find peace in Him. Describe how the *barack* of God has shown up in your life?

___

___

___

___

___

4. Another word for blessed is *asher*. Asher is a blessing that comes from walking in the ways of God, even when it is not comfortable to do so. Describe how the asher of God has shown up in your life?

___

_____

_____

_____

_____

5. Do you find it difficult to walk in the ways of God, even though you know it will yield blessings? Explain.

_____

_____

_____

_____

_____

6. What does fearing the LORD mean?

_____

_____

_____

_____

7. What does fearing the LORD look like?

_____

_____

_____

8. How can fathers use this lesson to make a difference in the lives of their children and future generations?

_____

_____

_____

_____

_____

Closing Prayer:

Father God, I worship you because you are God alone. There is no one greater than you. You are the center of my life and the giver of all blessings. Please forgive me, Father, for all the times I got caught up in my material blessings without focusing on the One who blesses. I thank you, LORD, for the opportunity to praise you, even on my way to deliverance, for I know that as long as I am connected to you, you will keep me in perfect peace. Now, LORD, help me to be productive, producing good fruit in my faith, in my household, and in my community. In Jesus' name, I pray. Hallelujah and amen.

Homework:

Use the following blank pages to journal your thoughts on this lesson throughout the week. Below are some tools to use as writing prompts to help you get started.

Answer this question - How can I apply this lesson to my everyday life?

Men - Reflect on all the ways you can be more productive and bear more fruit. Write down ways you plan on contributing more to your faith, family and future.

Women - Reflect on a man in your life (past or present), and jot down ways you can speak words of affirmation to let him know he is:

- Needed in his children's lives
- Accountable for his role in child-rearing
- Irreplaceable in his children's lives
- Responsible for making sacrifices for the sake of his children
- An effective father who will be rewarded by God

(See pages 38 and 39 in Bonded Love.)

LET'S JOURNAL!

Week 5

BEFORE WE SEPARATE, LET'S COMMUNICATE

Key Scripture: Song of Solomon 1:7-12, 5:10-16

Focal Verse: "His mouth is most sweet: yea, he is altogether lovely. This is my beloved, and this is my friend, O daughters of Jerusalem." – *vs. 5:16*

Overview:

In this lesson, you will:

- Learn to communicate with your spouse, even when it is difficult
- Understand the importance of communication and the dire consequences of not doing so
- Begin to make compliments a habitual part of your communication with your spouse

Lesson:

In 2007, Tyler Perry produced a movie titled, "Why Did I Get Married?" It is about four married couples who vacationed together in the snowy mountains of Colorado for a week of fun, laughs and reconnection. In this movie, we see how no marriage is above experiencing difficulties. While each has its own trials, we get a close up on the communication style of Sheila and Mike, played by Jill Scott and Richard T. Jones. Sheila is a woman who is overweight. Mike belittles his wife at every opportunity and speaks negatively to her and others about her looks. He even brags about making his wife drive to the mountains in inclement weather because she could not fit in an airplane seat, while he flies there with his mistress. While the movie is a work of fiction for entertainment purposes only, there are some wives out there (husbands too) who have experienced these same types of insults and negative comments in their marriage. If we are not careful, harsh and degrading communication – or even the absence of talking to one another about issues - can lead to a separation.

In Song of Solomon, we see a different kind of communication - words meant to build up and not tear down. King Solomon and his wife, the Shulamite woman, loved each other. It was evident in how they spoke to one another. He told his wife she was most beautiful, exciting and lovely. She described her husband as dark and dazzling, better than 10,000 others, black wavy hair, sparkling eyes, smelling good, and desirable in every way (NLT). The admiration between these two was endless. This young couple were not just lovers; they were also friends. How much more wonderful would your marriage be if you had a strong friendship? Or, if you compliment instead of condemn?

Read Song of Solomon 1:7-12 and 5:10-16

Questions for Discussion:

1. What are some examples of the ideal ways to communicate with your spouse? Use Solomon and the Shulamite woman as an example to get you started.

_____

_____

_____

_____

_____

2. Why is it difficult for some people to have courageous conversations – talking about those uncomfortable topics – in their marriage?

_____

_____

_____

_____

_____

3. A lack of communication can cause a separation between two people long before a physical or legal separation. What are some examples of how two people can be separated prior to a legal separation or divorce?

_____

_____

_____

_____

_____

4. Scripture gives us a recipe for enjoying life and seeing many happy days: keep your tongue from speaking evil

and your lips from telling lies (I Peter 3:10). What are some ways we speak evil to our spouse, and what are the potential consequences of our actions?

_____

_____

_____

_____

_____

5. Below are five reasons why we need to talk to each other. After each reason, give an example of how the relationship can deteriorate without constant and positive communication.

If you do not talk, you will drift apart.

Example: _____

_____

_____

_____

_____

Problems do not disappear just because you do not talk about them.

Example: _____

_____

_____

_____

_____

Talking gives touching more meaning.

Example: _____

_____

_____

_____

_____

Resentment will build up and fester if you do not talk.

Example: _____

_____

_____

_____

_____

Relationships are about deposits and withdrawals. If you try to make withdrawals without making any deposits (communication), it will not be good.

Example: _____

_____

_____

_____

_____

6. We should practice positive communication even if we think our spouse does not deserve it. Can you name a

time when God covered you with grace and did something positive for you, even when you did not deserve it?

_____

_____

_____

_____

_____

Closing Prayer:

Father God, I worship you today because you are Jehovah-Shalom. You are my peace. No matter what is happening all around me, no matter what is happening in my life, no matter what is happening in the world, your presence brings me peace. LORD, please forgive me for any time I have communicated with others in a way that was not pleasing to you. Thank you for showing me an example in Solomon and his wife of how to better communicate. I pray, Father God, you help me do my part in incorporating healthy conversations to bring about peace in my household. Help me to give more grace and less criticism. In Jesus' name, I pray. Hallelujah and amen.

Homework:

Use the following blank pages to journal your thoughts on this lesson throughout the week. Below are some tools to use as writing prompts to help you get started.

Answer this question - How can I apply this lesson to my everyday life?

For married couples: Communication should be about complimenting, admiring, showing affection, and being positive toward each other. If you are on the verge of a separation, write down your thoughts on how a lack of positive communication is contributing to the downfall of your relationship.

Perhaps, you are not heading toward a separation. Maybe you want to take preventive measures to fine-tune your marriage. Take time to practice incorporating the different communication techniques above throughout the week.

For singles: Separations can also occur between friends and family. Write down your thoughts on how a lack of positive communication is contributing to or contributed in the past to the downfall of those relationships.

LET'S JOURNAL!

Week 6

I'M IN THE FAMILY TOO

Key Scripture: Matthew 1:1-17

Focal Verse: "So all the generations from Abraham to David are fourteen generations; and from David until the carrying away into Babylon are fourteen generations; and from the carrying away into Babylon unto Christ are fourteen generations. – *vs. 17*

Overview:

In this lesson, you will:

- Understand how God develops His people who are waiting on His promises
- See how unlikely people can be in the family of Jesus Christ
- Learn how God's faithfulness still reigns in the midst of your failures

Lesson:

Tracing genealogy has become prevalent over the years amongst curious individuals looking to find answers about their family history and identity. Henry Louis Gates, Jr., a renowned Harvard scholar, has popularized this familial exploration with his weekly show, "Finding Your Roots." This series focuses on celebrities, as Gates helps them trace their ancestry as far as available information allows. His famous guests are fascinated to find out about some of the characters tucked away in their family tree. Some learn they have royal roots. Others learn they have African DNA. Gates pieces colorful stories together from his findings. On past shows, he has revealed family secrets such as who were outlaws, slave traders, pioneers, murderers, and – straight out of a Jerry Springer show – who is not the daddy!

Similar to "Finding Your Roots," we get a close look at the genealogy of another popular figure in the book of Matthew – The family tree of Jesus Christ. Matthew traces His lineage from Abraham (whom God promised would be a father of many nations) through to His birth. Dividing the time period into three sections, Matthew lets us know there are 14 generations from Abraham to David, 14 generations from David to the exile to Babylon, and 14 generations from the exile to the Messiah. Within the generations, we see familiar names, some with a checkered past. Jesus, our Redeemer, had family members who had some epic failures. But, despite their failures, they were still apart of His family. Because of His saving power and redeeming faithfulness, God includes unlikely people to be a part of His pedigree. If you believe that, you can also say, "I'm in the family too!"

Read Matthew 1:1-17

Questions for Discussion:

1. When God makes a promise, it always comes to pass. Sometimes, though, there is a delay in receiving His promise or blessing. It may even show up in future generations. Looking at Jesus' genealogy, list some examples of God's promises coming to fruition after a delay.

_____

_____

_____

_____

_____

2. Jesus had some family members who were impatient, much like us sometimes. They wanted their promised blessings to happen in their time instead of God's. What negative effects can occur when we do not wait on God's timing?

_____

_____

_____

_____

_____

3. What happens when you are waiting on God's promise, but your situation gets worse while you are waiting?

_____

_____

_____

_____

_____

4. God often takes his time delivering us from situations or giving us what He has promised. If this is your experience, think about a time when God was developing, maturing or strengthening you spiritually during your wait. Explain what you have learned.

_____

_____

_____

_____

_____

5. Jesus' genealogy shows us that we can be in His family regardless of our reputation, race or rank. Match the family member listed in Matthew with the correct characteristic.

Murderer: _____

Prostitute: _____

Liar: _____

Adulterer: _____

Fornicator: _____

Gentile: _____

Enslaved: _____

6. What advice would you give someone who says they cannot join the body of Christ because of their past or because they need to "get right" first before making that commitment?

_____
_____
_____
_____
_____

7. Even when we mess up, God is still faithful to us. Why do you believe He remains faithful to us, just as He did with Jesus' ancestors?

_____
_____
_____
_____
_____

8. How has God shown up for you, despite your failures?

_____
_____
_____
_____
_____

Closing Prayer:

Father God, I worship you because you are Abba. You are the head of my home and my life. There is no father greater than You. Just like earthly fathers who sense when their children are doing wrong, I know you know all my failures and shortcomings. Please forgive me, LORD, for not always living a life worthy of your faithfulness. I thank you for your bonded love that unites me with your family and for the sacrifice of Jesus on the cross. Now LORD, I pray you give me the wisdom to understand when you are trying to grow and develop me. Quiet my anxious spirit when I want immediate results. In Jesus' name, I pray. Hallelujah and amen.

Homework:

Use the following blank pages to journal your thoughts on this lesson throughout the week. Below are some tools to use as writing prompts to help you get started.

Answer this question - How can I apply this lesson to my everyday life?

Every family member has a role they play. The boss, the reliable one, the baby, the unmotivated one, the super spiritual one, the feisty one, etc. In the family of Christ, what is your role? Is there room for improvement in your role? How are you contributing to your Christian family?

LET'S JOURNAL!

Week 7

LESSONS FROM YOUNG LOVERS

Key Scripture: Matthew 1:18-25

Focal Verse: "But while he thought on these things, behold, the angel of the LORD appeared unto him in a dream, saying, Joseph, thou son of David, fear not to take unto thee Mary they wife: for that which is conceived in her is of the Holy Ghost." – *vs. 20*

Overview:

In this lesson, you will:

- Understand the importance of listening to God's voice
- Recognize the importance of being evenly yoked in your relationship
- See how God can turn messy situations in a marriage around

Lesson:

Men, imagine you have a fiancé, and you just found out she is pregnant. Since you two have not been physically intimate because you were saving yourselves for marriage, you know the baby is not yours. I am sure you would feel betrayed, hurt, angry, fearful, and embarrassed all at the same time. "How could she step out on me?" "Why would she do this to someone she loves?" "Who has she been with?" "What will I tell my family?" "Are my friends going to laugh at me?" "How can I show my face in public again?"

Would these be the kinds of questions swirling around in your head?

Well, imagine how Joseph felt in Matthew 1, as the Bible describes Mary's pregnancy. Joseph and Mary were espoused, (engaged) to be married, but before they could get married, Mary, who was a virgin, became pregnant. Joseph was obviously fearful and upset by this because the Bible tells us he decided to break off the engagement. That is when God stepped into this messy situation. God dispatched an angel who appeared to Joseph in a dream to let him know he should not be afraid because the child within Mary was conceived by the Holy Spirit. Heeding the angel's instructions, Joseph married his young bride as planned and named their son Jesus.

In this Scripture, we get a glimpse into Joseph's character through the decision he was contemplating, the dream he had when he encountered the angel, the distress he experienced from the situation and wanting to quietly rectify it, and his demonstration of obedience and trust when he did as the angel of the LORD instructed him to do. This story demonstrates how God's perfect plan will go forth when we listen and obey His word.

Read Matthew 1:18-25

Questions for Discussion:

1. In this story, an angel of the LORD appeared to Joseph in a dream as he was contemplating a tough decision. Has God ever used someone to deliver a message to you? If so, did you act upon it? Why or why not?

_____

_____

_____

_____

_____

2. What is your process when you must make difficult and life-changing decisions, either as a couple or individual? Is God a part of that process?

_____

_____

_____

_____

_____

3. Do you struggle when your decisions are based on God's will instead of your own will? Explain.

_____

_____

_____

_____

_____

4. Joseph decided to listen to God instead of quietly calling off his engagement to Mary. What would have happened to

the prophesy from Isaiah 100 years earlier (Isaiah 7:14) if Joseph made a different decision?

_____
_____
_____
_____
_____

5. The Bible describes Joseph as a just man; a righteous man. It describes Mary as a virgin; highly favored; blessed. What can these two young lovers teach us about being equally yoked? About showing restraint?

_____
_____
_____
_____
_____

6. Mary had Jesus on the inside of her, but it did not stop this couple from having relationship issues. What can we learn from Joseph and Mary about Christian couples experiencing problems?

_____
_____
_____

_____

_____

7. Jesus can see you through any issue, problem, difficulty or challenge in your marriage or relationship. What are some steps you can take now on the road to recovery from a failing to a flourishing relationship?

_____

_____

_____

_____

_____

Closing Prayer:

Father God, I worship you because you are Jehovah-Nissi. You are my banner. There is no one more powerful than you. Please forgive me for any decision I have ever made that went against your will and your word. Forgive me for any bad decision I may have even contemplated. I thank you, LORD, for keeping me in the midst of some relationship storms. As I run this race in my marriage, my relationship, and in life, I pray you give me victory against anything or anyone who comes up against me and your will for my life. In Jesus' name, I pray. Hallelujah and amen.

Homework:

Use the following blank pages to journal your thoughts on this lesson throughout the week. Below are some tools to use as writing prompts to help you get started.

Answer this question - How can I apply this lesson to my everyday life?

You can glean lessons from Joseph and Mary on how God can put marriages and relationships back together again. But sometimes, we need trusted accountability partners in our circle we can lean on. If you are married, list other Christian couples with longevity whom you can partner with for spiritual guidance.

Make a list of tears in your relationship. Pray over it and ask God to mend those areas that are torn.

If you are not married, make a list of trusted Christian friends or family members whom you can partner with for spiritual guidance.

LET'S JOURNAL!

Week 8

THAT KIND OF LOVE

Key Scripture: Romans 5:5-11

Focal Verse: "But God commendeth his love toward us, in that, while we were yet sinners, Christ died for us." – *vs. 8*

Overview:

In this lesson, you will:

- Understand what God's love looks like in the past and present
- Learn what justification is and the benefits of being justified
- Explore the importance of pouring the love of God into others

Lesson:

"The 5 love Languages: The Secret to Love That Lasts," is a New York Times bestselling book by Gary Chapman. In it, he explains how communicating love to someone or receiving love from someone falls into five categories. The book helps readers determine how they want to receive love from their partner and how they should be giving love back in return. It has assisted millions of people who have found themselves with an empty love tank. You can ask yourself, "How do I know he/she loves me?" The answer might be, "because he holds my hand or buys me gifts." Or, maybe the answer is, "because she speaks positively to me and spends time with me." Alternatively, "because he washes my car and runs my bath water when I need to relax." This may be what the love of a devoted spouse looks like who is speaking your love language, but it does not measure up to the incomparable love of God.

Romans 5 describes that kind of love from God that is abundant and generous. It will never disappoint us and will never run out. Whatever our love language is, God decided to show us mercy because, while we were weak and sinful, Jesus took on the burden of our sins and nailed them to the cross on Calvary. This sacrificial act made us exempt from the punishment we deserved. God bestowed grace upon us instead. Because we are believers, He forgives our sin and saves us from condemnation.

Who can keep that kind of love to themselves? Remember, "The 5 Love Languages" is about receiving *and* giving. Since God's love is so abundant, we have an opportunity to share that love with others so they may bask in His overflow too. When someone has an encounter with us, they ought to sense we are indwelled with God's Holy Spirit by how we treat them and others.

Read Romans 5:5-11

Questions For Discussion:

1. What did God do for us in the past to show us how much He loves us?

   _____
   _____
   _____

_____

_____

2. What can we do for God now to show Him how much we love Him?

_____

_____

_____

_____

_____

3. Justification is defined as the act of God whereby humankind is made or accounted *just* or free from guilt or penalty of sin. According to vs. 6, why did humankind need justification?

_____

_____

_____

_____

_____

4. Below are five benefits to being justified or saved from condemnation. Next to each one, describe how it applies to your life today.

Peace with God: _____

_____

_____

_____

_____

Access to God: _____

_____

_____

_____

Assurance of God: _____

_____

_____

Indwelled by God through His Holy Spirit: _____

_____

_____

_____

_____

Preserved by God: _____

_____

_____

_____

_____

5. The love of God controls us. Give an example of how God's love has controlled your tongue, attitude or actions.

_____

_____

_____

_____

_____

6. The love of God convicts us. Give an example of how God's love has convicted you before.

_____

_____

_____

_____

_____

7. Love is an action word, and the Bible talks about it extensively. In fact, Jesus said the greatest commandments are to love God and love our neighbors (Mark 12:28-31). List some ways we can love our neighbors, not because of who they are or what they do for us, but because of the love of God.

_____

_____

_____

_____

_____

Closing Prayer:

Father God, I worship you because you are Elohim. You are God, and you are a loving God. Forgive me, LORD, for my sin that keeps me from getting close to you. As David has said, wash me thoroughly from mine iniquity, and cleanse me from my sin. I thank you for your son, Jesus, and His sacrifice on the cross. I thank you that my sin died on the cross with Him. I thank you for raising Him from the dead with all power in His hands. I thank you for your impunity that comes from your love. Now, LORD, I pray that you continue to preserve me as I walk in love. In Jesus' name, I pray. Hallelujah and amen.

Homework:

Use the following blank pages to journal your thoughts on this lesson throughout the week. Below are some tools to use as writing prompts to help you get started.

Answer this question - How can I apply this lesson to my everyday life?

Make a list of how you plan to show love this week to the following people:

- Family member
- Co-worker
- Pastor
- Stranger

LET'S JOURNAL!

Week 9

ENDLESS LOVE

Key Scripture: Romans 8:35-39

Focal Verses: "For I am persuaded, that neither death, nor life, nor angels, nor principalities, nor powers, nor things present, nor things to come, Nor height, nor depth, nor any other creature, shall be able to separate us from the love of God, which is in Christ Jesus our Lord." – *vs. 38-39*

Overview:

In this lesson, you will:

- Learn that God's love for us is an endless love
- Explore different scenarios that try to separate you from God's endless love
- Gain confidence in your bonded love with Christ

Lesson:

The Bible demonstrates so many different ways God shows us His love. Even from the beginning of time, He made humankind in His own image and blessed them (Genesis 1:28). He also established a rainbow as a sign of His covenant with Noah and every living creature that He would not destroy the earth with a flood anymore for perpetual generations (Genesis 9:11-13). The love of God also brought the children of Israel out of Egyptian bondage (Exodus 14:30). Then, over in the New Testament, Jesus tells us God loved the world so much, He sacrificed His very own Son so that we would have an everlasting life (John 3:16). By the time we get to the book of Romans, we learn that God's love is inseparable.

This is good news for us because we certainly go through some challenges in life that try to separate us from God's love. Even when we get distracted with life's chaos and forget to check in with God, He is still there. When we are under attack, He is still there. All we have to do is look back over our lives. If the occurrences of our past – which tried to destroy us - did not separate us from God's love, you know for certain that in your *right now* situations or your future predicaments, God's endless love will be right there with you in the midst of what you are going through.

Read Romans 8:35-39

Questions for Discussion:

1. Have you ever felt separated or even abandoned by God because of your struggles or failures? Explain.

_____
_____
_____
_____
_____

2. Verse 35 starts off with a question: (NLT) "Can anything ever separate us from Christ's love?" By the time we get to verse 38, we get the answer to the question: Nothing can! How can we be sure of this answer?

_____

_____

_____

_____

_____

3. Paul noted several crises that can interrupt our lives. Make a list of those things found in vs. 35. Take one you have endured and explain how you felt about God's presence in your situation.

_____

_____

_____

_____

_____

4. In verse 36, it says, "...We are killed all the day long; we are accounted as sheep for the slaughter." What does that mean to you?

_____

_____

_____

_____

_____

5. Often, we pray for God's deliverance *from* various situations, but God allows us to go *through* them anyway. If He loves us, why do you think He allows us to go through tribulation?

_____

_____

_____

_____

_____

6. In verse 37, Paul said we are more than conquerors in all these things – meaning, in all the tribulations and struggles we go through. What is the difference between being a conqueror and being more than a conqueror?

_____

_____

_____

_____

_____

7. We do not always feel victorious while we are going through struggles. How can we be like Paul and declare we are more than conquerors, even when we do not see a way out?

_____

_____

_____

_____

_____

8. In verse 38, Paul said he was persuaded. That means he was convinced without a shadow of doubt. Why do you think Paul was so confident, so sure, that nothing shall be able to separate us from the love of God?

_____

_____

_____

_____

_____

Closing Prayer:

Father God, I worship you because you are El Olam, the Everlasting God. You are Alpha and Omega. LORD, I'm sorry for the times I made the wrong choice when struggling to do what was right. Please forgive me. I thank you for being a gracious God, one who walks with me through every obstacle of my life. You have delivered me time and time again, and I say thank you. Now, LORD, when I get weak and my burdens get too heavy, I pray you remind me of how you've kept me in the past and how you can see me to victory in the future. Thank you for your endless love. In Jesus' name, I pray. Hallelujah and amen.

Homework:

Use the following blank pages to journal your thoughts on this lesson throughout the week. Below are some tools to use as writing prompts to help you get started.

Answer this question - How can I apply this lesson to my everyday life?

Make a list of situations you are experiencing where you need victory in your life. Meditate and pray on it this week. If you need to be persuaded of God's ability to walk you through it, make another list of situations He has brought you through in the past.

LET'S JOURNAL!

Week 10

LOVE'S POWER OVER ALL THINGS

Key Scripture: I Corinthians 13:1-7

Focal Verse: "Beareth all things, believeth all things, hopeth all things, endureth all things." – *vs. 7*

Overview:

In this lesson, you will:

- Understand how powerful God's love is
- Know when to apply God's love
- Appreciate your circumstances when you have God confidence

Lesson:

Those who are fans of superheroes know they hold extraordinary powers. Marvel Comics has characters such as Black Panther, Spider-Man, Iron Man, Captain America, Thor, Doctor Strange, and Hulk. Maybe you are a fan of DC Comics and movies. That means you enjoy characters such as Superman, Batman, Wonder Woman, Green Lantern, The Flash, Aquaman, Cyborg, and Black Lightning. In following these characters, you know humankind depends on them to use their remarkable powers to remedy dire circumstances. They are the good guys. They are deemed superheroes because of their love for and protection of humanity. This love covers all types of situations they may encounter. While these are fictional characters and scenarios, there is One who is all powerful in reality, and His love also covers us in all types of situations.

I Corinthians 13 opens up with stressing the importance of love. Paul lets us know that we can accomplish great things, but if we do not have love, we would be nothing. We could be the best linguist, have the gift of prophecy, understand all mysteries, have the biggest faith, and be the most charitable givers to the poor, but none of that means anything if we do not love others. Love never gives up, never loses faith, is always hopeful, and endures through every circumstance. That is the love in which we should operate from. That is the love God operates from, and His love has power over all things that may come up in our lives.

Read I Corinthians 13:1-7

Questions for Discussion:

1. Has your definition of love changed since the start of this study? If so, how?

   _____

   _____

   _____

   _____

   _____

2. Give an example of love in action.

   _____

   _____

3. What is the anatomy of love outlined in I Corinthians? (verses 4-7)

4. The Bible says love bears *all* things. What are some exceptions to this rule?

5. To bear all things means to have you covered in support – as in the weight of something heavy – without giving up or giving out. For example, Christ had to bear the cross for our sins. Name something else Christ decided to bear for you.

_____

_____

_____

_____

_____

6. Sometimes it is people who can be unbearable instead of situations. Give an example of how you can show the love of God to someone who seems unbearable.

_____

_____

_____

_____

_____

7. To believe all things means to seek the best in a person or predicament. That is what God does with us. Give an example of how God does this for you.

_____

_____

_____

_____

_____

8. If you believe all things, you could be described as an optimist. Do you believe God's love can shine through

imperfect people to demonstrate His power over all things? Explain.

_____

_____

_____

_____

_____

9. Do you ever have hope for a positive outcome in situations that feel hopeless, or do you get stressed out over what you do not know or see? Explain.

_____

_____

_____

_____

_____

10. If you ran a marathon and came in last place, you would still receive a finisher medal no matter how you placed. That is because you endured through the entire race and did not give up. Just like finishing a marathon, love endures all things. What helps you endure when you want to give up during tough circumstances?

_____

_____

_____

_____

_____

Closing Prayer:

Father God, I worship you because you are El Elyon, The Most High God. At the center of your infinite power is love. Forgive me, LORD, for the times I did not seek your face when dealing with life's challenges, even though I knew your love has brought me through before. I thank you for the storms that have come my way, because without them, I would not know the magnitude of your power. I pray that you continue to build my God confidence because I know you cause everything to work together for my good. I love you, God. In Jesus' name, I pray. Hallelujah and amen.

Homework:

Use the following blank pages to journal your thoughts on this lesson throughout the week. Below are some tools to use as writing prompts to help you get started.

Answer this question - How can I apply this lesson to my everyday life?

Has God ever worked anything out for your good? If so, use it as a testimony to share with someone this week. Pray to God that He strategically puts someone in your path who needs to hear it.

LET'S JOURNAL!

_____
_____
_____
_____
_____
_____
_____
_____
_____
_____
_____
_____
_____
_____
_____
_____
_____
_____
_____
_____
_____
_____
_____
_____

Week 11

LOVE'S POWER OVER TIME

Key Scripture: I Corinthians 13, 14:1

Focal Verse: "Love never fails. But whether there are prophecies, they will fail; whether there are tongues, they will cease; whether there is knowledge, it will vanish away." -vs. 13:8 (NKJV)

Overview:

In this lesson, you will:

- Understand how God's love never fails
- Recognize the priority, the practice, and the permanence of love
- Learn to pursue love

Lesson:

We can experience weather-related storms that are so bad, the power will go out. This could be a hurricane, tornado, blizzard, or ice storm. Even though the power may fail, the One who controls the storms has love that never fails.

You can buy a brand-new car off the lot of your favorite dealership, but over time, that car's engine will fail, but God's love will never fail or lose value over time, unlike the car.

You can be in an ideal marriage, and overtime, experience mounting problems that cause it to fail. The love may eventually run out, but God's love is never extinguished. It never fails.

Paul makes this point very clear in I Corinthians 13. In verse 8, he says plainly, love never fails. This was a direct message to the Church of Corinth because the church was experiencing some issues. Paul wanted to let them know that God's love still covered them, even when they messed up. And that is a message for everyone reading this today. It seems like an impossible feat to do the right thing all the time. But, the Bible tells us that the things which are impossible with men are possible with God (Luke 18:27). It is possible for the power of His love to cover the Corinthians long ago, and it can cover you today. That is love's power over time. Because love is the greatest (I Corinthians 13:13), God wants us to make it a priority in our lives. We can put this in practice by showing agape love – an unselfish concern for the welfare of others – without motivation. It will stand the test of time when all else fails.

Read I Corinthians 13, 14:1

Questions for Discussion:

1. In the church of Corinth, the people were sanctified saints, set apart for God's purpose, but they still had trouble in the church. This lets us know we are not exempt from troubles, conflicts and temptations either, even if we are believers. Think of a time you had conflict with someone, whether it was a co-worker, family member, stranger in traffic, or another believer. How did you resolve the conflict?

_____

_____

_____

_____

_____

2. Why is love so important (verses 1-3)?

_____

_____

_____

_____

_____

3. As Christians, we ought to make love a priority. How can we be more intentional about representing love and showing love to others?

_____

_____

_____

_____

_____

4. In the previous week, we looked at what love is as outlined in verses 4-7. Give an example of the following attributes of love:

Patient love: _____

_____

_____

_____

_____

Kind love: _____

_____

_____

_____

_____

Truthful love: _____

_____

_____

_____

_____

Bearing love: _____

_____

_____

_____

_____

Believing love: _____

_____

_____

_____

_____

Hopeful love: _____

_____

_____

_____

_____

Enduring love: _____

_____

_____

_____

_____

5. Love should be the center of whatever we do for the church or for others. Give an example of what it looks like when we do for others or the church and our motives *are not* rooted in love.

_____

_____

_____

_____

_____

6. God's love does not change over time. Its power does not weaken as time passes. That is not in His character. Is consistency an important trait to you when evaluating the relationships in your life? Explain.

_____
_____
_____
_____
_____

7. I Corinthians 14:1 tells us to follow after love and let it be our highest goal. How can we achieve this?

_____
_____
_____
_____
_____

Closing Prayer:

Father God, I worship you because you are Adonai, my LORD and Master. You are the One who leads and guides me in love. You are the head of my life. I pray for forgiveness, LORD, for any time I may have been jealous, boastful, selfish or rude. I thank you for keeping me covered in grace. I thank you for your love that never runs out, even when I try to run away from you. Now, LORD, please teach me your ways. Help me to have a deeper and consistent love with you and others. In Jesus' name, I pray. Hallelujah and amen.

Homework:

Use the following blank pages to journal your thoughts on this lesson throughout the week. Below are some tools to use as writing prompts to help you get started.

Answer this question - How can I apply this lesson to my everyday life?

If you plant an apple tree from a seedling, it will eventually grow and produce fruit. The Bible tells us the Holy Spirit produces fruit in our lives, and one of those fruits is love (Galatians 5:22-23). What must you do to nourish that fruit - that love – so it may grow and supply an abundant, regenerating harvest?

LET'S JOURNAL!

Week 12

THE THRILL IS GONE

Key Scripture: Revelation 2:1-7

Focal Verse: "Nevertheless I have somewhat against thee, because thou hast left they first love." - *vs. 4*

Overview:

In this lesson, you will:

- Understand why God told John to write a letter to the church in Ephesus

- Learn best practices for having difficult conversations with people

- Gain a recipe for getting back on track when you fall short in your relationship with God and others

Lesson:

B.B. King was a world-renowned blues singer, songwriter, guitar player, and record producer before his death in 2015. Just as popular as his identifiable sound was his guitar, affectionately named Lucille. With more than 50 albums under his belt beginning in the 1940s, he earned the title, *King of the Blues.* Some could even call him the G.O.A.T. of blues. That's right – the Greatest of All Time! With all his popular tracks admired by so many, he was probably best known for "The Thrill Is Gone."

The thrill is gone
The thrill is gone away
The thrill is gone baby
The thrill is gone away
You know you done me wrong baby
And you'll be sorry someday

That is the sentiment we find in Revelation 2. The Apostle John wrote a letter to the church in Ephesus because the thrill was gone. The church leaders and the people in Ephesus knew the LORD because Paul had preached the gospel there. They loved God at one time and did not tolerate evil. The Ephesians worked diligently and patiently until something shifted. They had fallen. As B.B. King once said, "You know you done me wrong baby." They did wrong by becoming a loveless church. But, unlike King's one verse which says, "It's gone away for good," God allowed the Ephesians to repent and get back on track. And that is a lesson for us today. If we remember what our relationship used to be – whether with God, spouse, friend, family, or someone else significant in our lives – repent for our faults and turn away from them, and begin to do those things we did in the beginning, we will be victorious.

Read Revelation 2:1-7

Questions for Discussion:

The Apostle John sent word to the church in Ephesus. It was a message from God. The first thing he told them was, "I know all the things you do." If God made a list of all the things we do, would He be pleased or disappointed? Explain.

_____

_____

_____

_____

_____

2. John lodged a complaint against the church in Ephesus, but he started with a soft approach first. He commended the church before he condemned it. What did John say the church did right? (vs. 2)

_____

_____

_____

_____

_____

3. What did John say the church did wrong? (vs. 4)

_____

_____

_____

_____

_____

4. How do you think the Ephesians' actions affected the church body as a whole?

_____

_____

_____

_____

_____

5. Sometimes we act like the Ephesians and leave God. What do you think causes us to stray away from Him?

_____

_____

_____

_____

_____

6. Often, this scenario plays out in marriages and relationships too. We start out in love, then over time, it fizzles. Experts say poor communication is a leading cause of divorce. What can we learn about constructive communication from the Apostle John?

_____

_____

_____

_____

_____

7. The Ephesians worked diligently in the church for the LORD's sake, much like we do today. But the Bible tells us they left their first love. Have you ever been busy in the church but your service was void of love, emotion or devotion? Did you overcome it? If so, how?

_____

_____

_____

_____

_____

8. God does not move away from us. We move away from Him. But even though we stray, He gives us an opportunity to be reunited with His bonded love. What are the three things John told the church to do? (vs. 5)

_____

_____

_____

_____

_____

Closing Prayer:

Father God, I worship you because you are Yahweh, my LORD. You are omniscient – all knowing. Just like the Ephesians, you know all the things I do. Please forgive me for not being loving to you and others as I used to. Forgive me for doing those things I should not and neglecting those things I ought to do. LORD, I thank you for a second and third and fourth chance to get it right. Now LORD, please heal me in the areas where I'm fickle in my affections and service toward you. As I remember how it was in the beginning, help me to use that as fuel to reconnect. I love you, God. In Jesus' name, I pray. Hallelujah and amen.

Homework:

Use the following blank pages to journal your thoughts on this lesson throughout the week. Below are some tools to use as writing prompts to help you get started.

Answer this question - How can I apply this lesson to my everyday life?

For married couples who are struggling:

Take some time to remember how it was when you first fell in love with your spouse. Jot down some thoughts about why you fell in love. Then, repent for any part you played in the downfall of the marriage. Pray and ask God to strengthen your marriage, improve your communications, and fix anything else that is tearing it apart. Next, begin to redo those things you did in the beginning of the marriage, showing acts of love to your spouse. Write down the thoughtful actions you plan to take.

For saints in the church:

Take some time to remember how it was when you first fell in love with God. Jot down some thoughts about why you fell in love. What was going on in your life at the time of your salvation that drew you to Him? Make notes on all the ways you served Him and the church. Then, repent for turning your back on Him even though you knew better. Write down a plan on what you will do to draw closer to God's bonded love.

LET'S JOURNAL!

ABOUT THE AUTHOR

Damone Paul Johnson is a recognized teacher, preacher and author.

He is the senior Pastor of Metropolitan NTM Baptist Church in Upstate New York. As the lead shepherd since 2003, his transformational teachings continue to thrive amongst the intergenerational congregation which has grown in ministry and mission. Under his leadership, Metropolitan expanded its footprint in its beloved community and shaped a virtual church ministering to people around the world weekly on Facebook, YouTube, and the church's website.

Johnson is also the founder of DPJ Ministries, whose mission is to take the word of God to the world. The emphasis on Word and world, taking the Word – the Holy Bible – to the uttermost parts of the world.

He lives in Albany with the love of his life, his wife, Angela D. Johnson.

www.damonepauljohnson.com
Facebook: @dpjministries
Instagram: @dpjministries

OTHER BOOKS BY DAMONE PAUL JOHNSON

- "Bonded Love: How God's Love Shines Through Imperfect Relationships"
- "A Life Worth Rebuilding"
- "A Life Worth Rebuilding Study Guide"
- "Beyond the Grave Devotional"

www.ingramcontent.com/pod-product-compliance
Lightning Source LLC
Chambersburg PA
CBHW071006080526
44587CB00015B/2370